In this book, we're going to talk about Egyptian hieroglyphics. So, let's get right to it!

WHAT IS HIEROGLYPHICS?

Hieroglyphics is a complex system of writing. The Ancient Egyptians used a series of words that were drawn with pictures to communicate information about objects and ideas. The word "hieroglyphic" comes from the Greek words for "God's words" or "holy writings." It is a good description of their language, because the Egyptians thought that their writing was sacred. They began to develop this system of written communication around 3200 BC.

Book of the Dead

WRITING HIEROGLYPHICS
(WITH ACTUAL EXAMPLES!)

History Kids Books
Children's Ancient History

BABY PROFESSOR
EDUCATION KIDS

Speedy Publishing LLC

40 E. Main St. #1156

Newark, DE 19711

www.speedypublishing.com

Copyright 2017

All Rights reserved. No part of this book may be reproduced or used in any way or form or by any means whether electronic or mechanical, this means that you cannot record or photocopy any material ideas or tips that are provided in this book

Religion was very important to the life of the Ancient Egyptians and many of the most ancient hieroglyphics found were carved or painting on temples and tombs. They also used hieroglyphs to create their sacred books, such as the famous Book of the Dead.

At the beginning of the development of hieroglyphics, the basic language they used had hundreds of symbols and pictures, but it wasn't a strict translation of picture to meaning. It was also written with phonetic symbols that indicated how the words would sound when spoken. This combination of picture symbols for objects and picture symbols representing sounds makes the language complicated to decipher.

Hieroglyphics

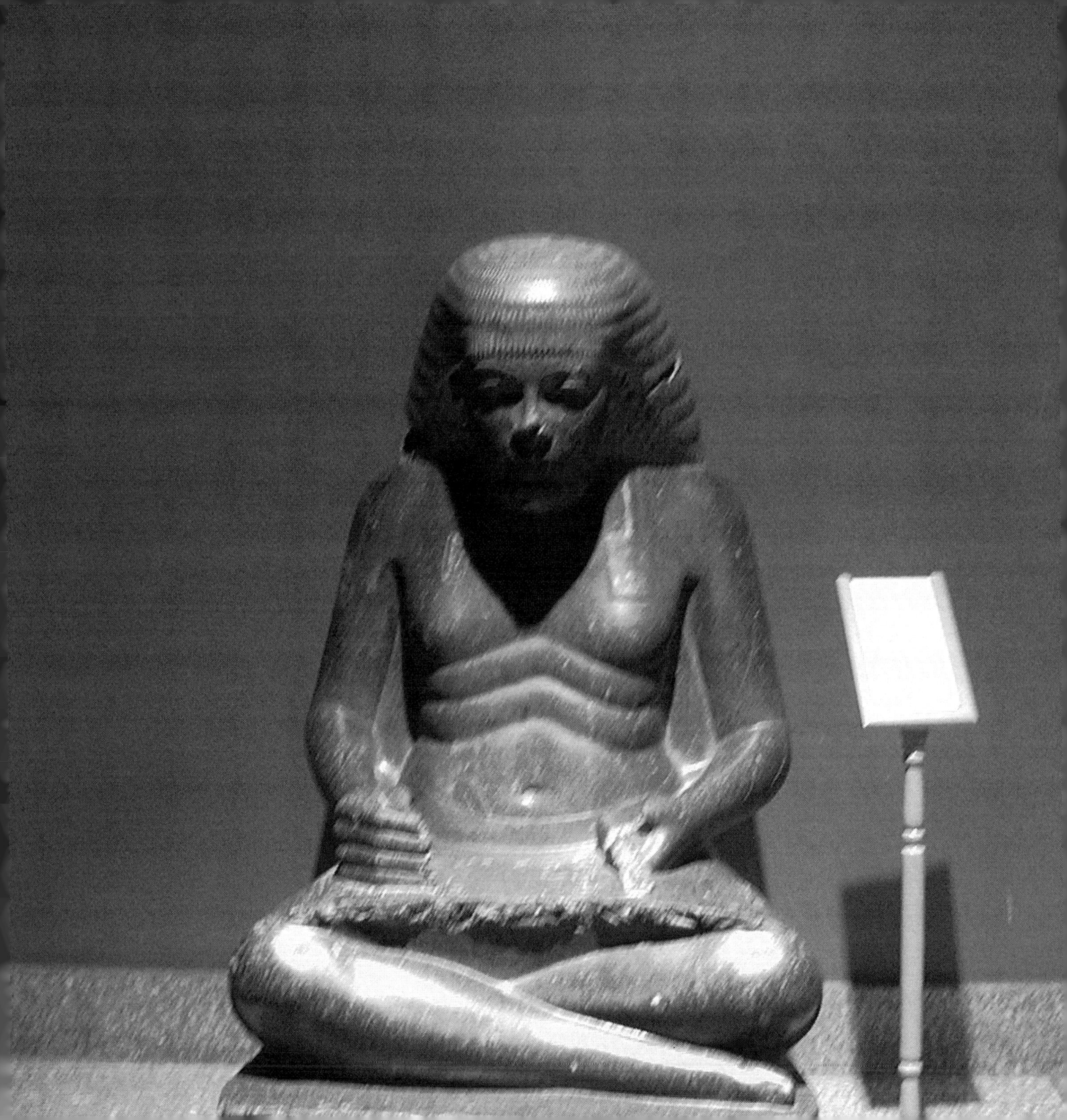

Because the Egyptian language was so difficult to read, only about 3% of the population ever learned to read. It also took a tremendous amount of effort to write. Even the scribes who had mastered the language found it tedious and time-consuming to write. Eventually, they developed a "shorthand" version of the language to speed things up!

THE THREE DIFFERENT CLASSES OF HIEROGLYPHS

Egyptologists have discovered that there are actually three different types of Egyptian hieroglyphs. To make matters even more complicated, some of the glyphs can be classified in more than one of these categories.

U.C. 16506.

ΜΕΝ | ΝΑΙ
ΔΙΟ | ΡΟΥ
ΚΗΡΥ | ΞΙΩ
ΑΥΤ | ΟΣ
ΕΥ

Ideograms

These hieroglyphs represent ideas instead of sounds. The symbols for man, woman, or the name of a god or ruler would be examples of ideograms.

Phonograms

Phonograms are symbols that signify a specific sound when a word or words are spoken. For example, in English, we have a phonogram for the long sound of "e" as in the word tree.

Egyptian Hieroglyphs

Determinatives

The determinatives were glyphs that weren't spoken. Their purpose was to make the meanings of combinations of symbols clearer. They also marked when a specific word had come to an end. This type of marking was definitely needed since the Egyptians didn't have any spaces in their writing. Words and sentences all ran on like an endless stream. They didn't use any punctuation either!

NO ONE SPEAKS THE EGYPTIAN LANGUAGE TODAY

There's a reason that no one speaks the Egyptian language today. Modern scholars can decipher the written language, but no one knows how the original Egyptian language was spoken. The Egyptians didn't use any vowels in their written language at all! Because of this, no one knows how the language was actually pronounced or spoken.

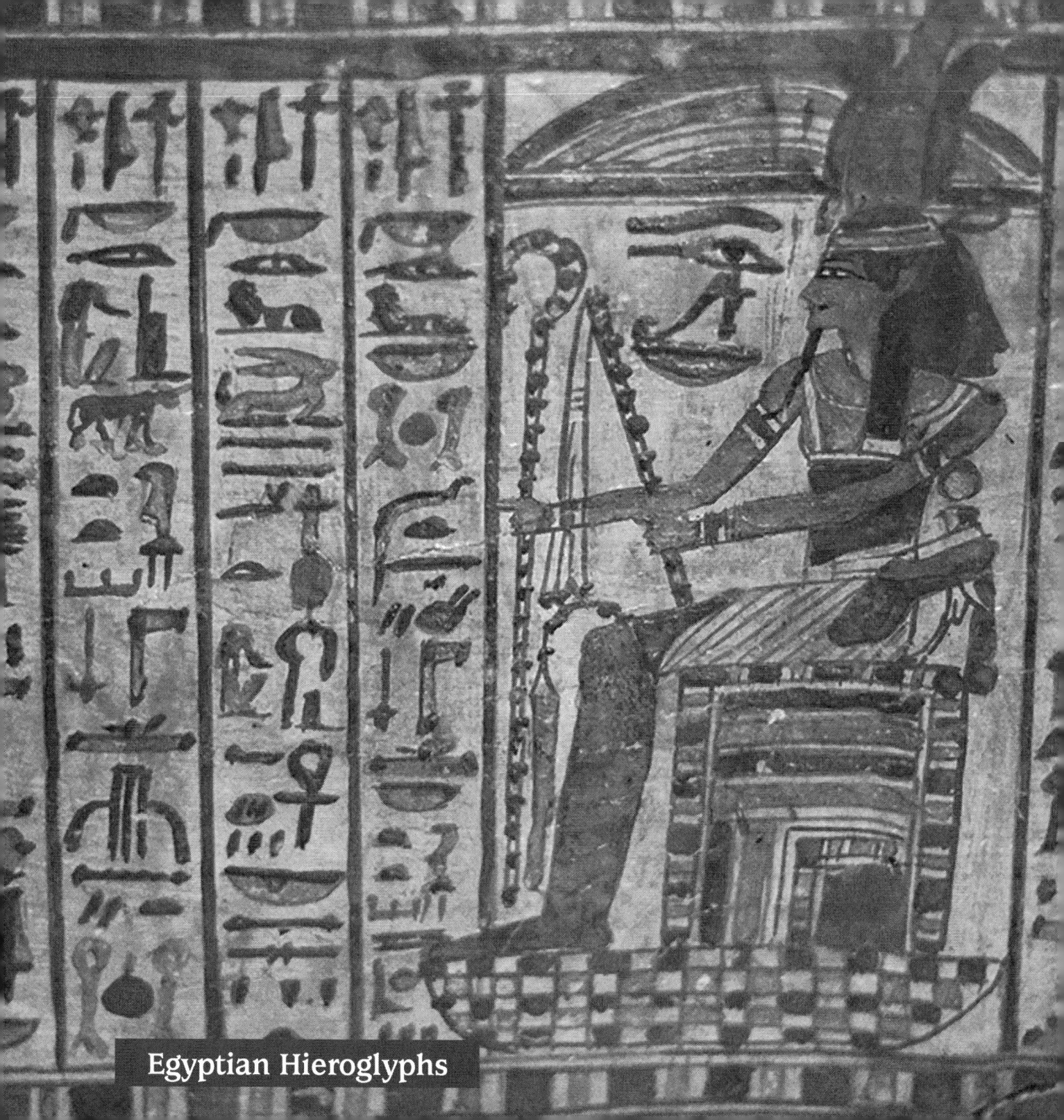

Egyptian Hieroglyphs

Some words used the same exact set of consonants so there were determinatives positioned at the end of the words to indicate which meaning the glyphs had. For example, if a name was written, there was a glyph showing a man or a woman so it was clear whether the name represented a male or a female.

WHICH DIRECTION WERE HIEROGLYPHS READ ON THE PAGE?

In the English language, we read across the page from left to right, but not all languages are like this. Hieroglyphics can be written and read either horizontally or vertically.

Egyptian Hieroglyphs

They can also be read from right to left or from left to right. You can tell which way the symbols were supposed to be read from the way they face. If the signs face the right direction, then they are meant to be read from right to left. If they face the left direction, then they are meant to be read from left to right.

THE NEED FOR BALANCE

Balance and harmony were very important to the Egyptian culture. Some objects had a series of inscriptions that could be read in more than one direction. For example, if there was an inscription on one side of a window, the Egyptians would create a balanced inscription for the other side as well.

Karnak

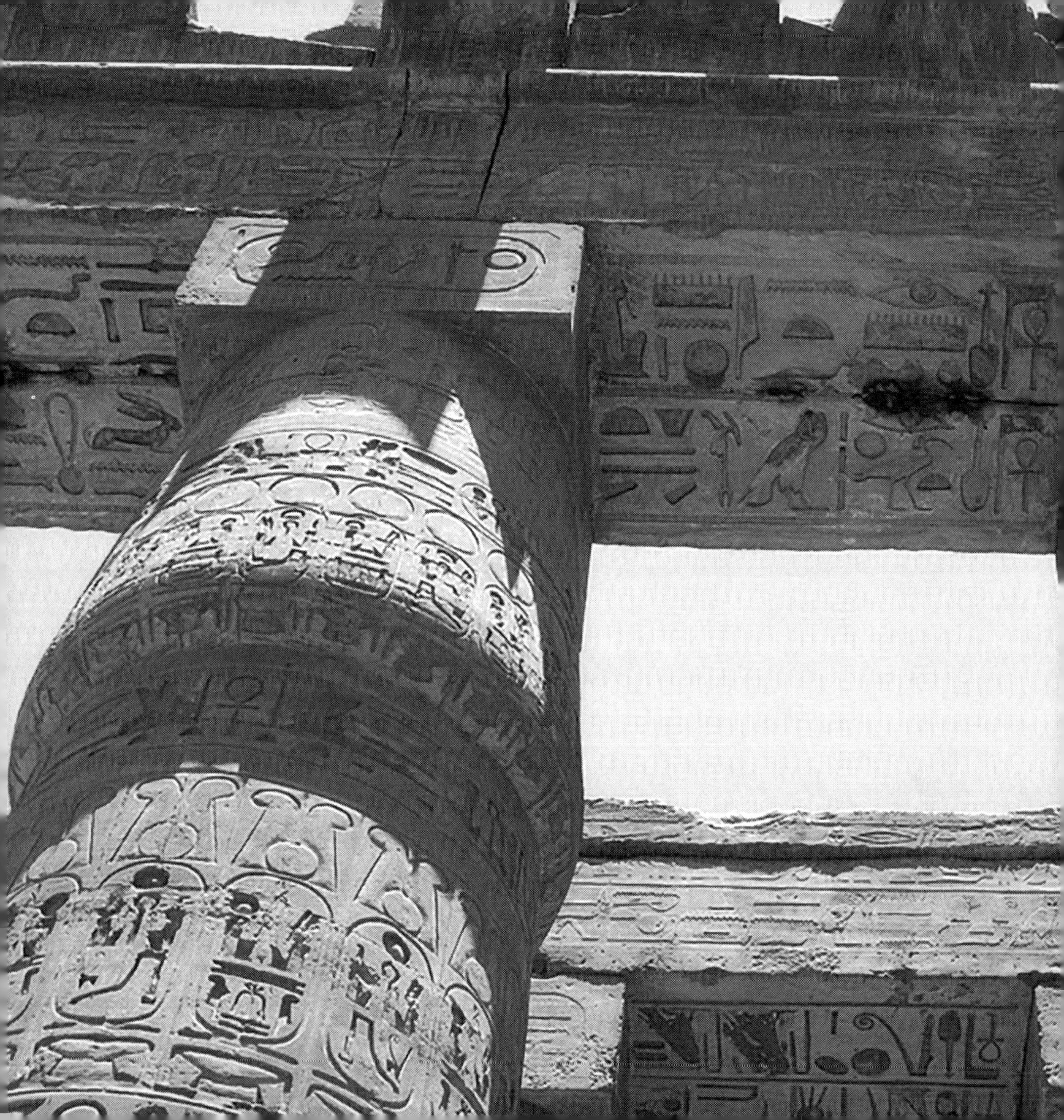

They rarely left empty spaces, but instead they stacked their writings leaving no spaces between individual words or groups of sentences. Hieroglyphics was a form of art, so it was important to the Egyptians for their writing to look as beautiful as a painting.

A BRIEF HISTORY OF HIEROGLYPHICS

There's evidence that the use of hieroglyphics began as early as 3200 BC. At the start there were about 700 glyphs, but by 300 BC, there were more than 6,000 signs and symbols. Many of the signs were developed from things that the Egyptians viewed in nature or in their daily life.

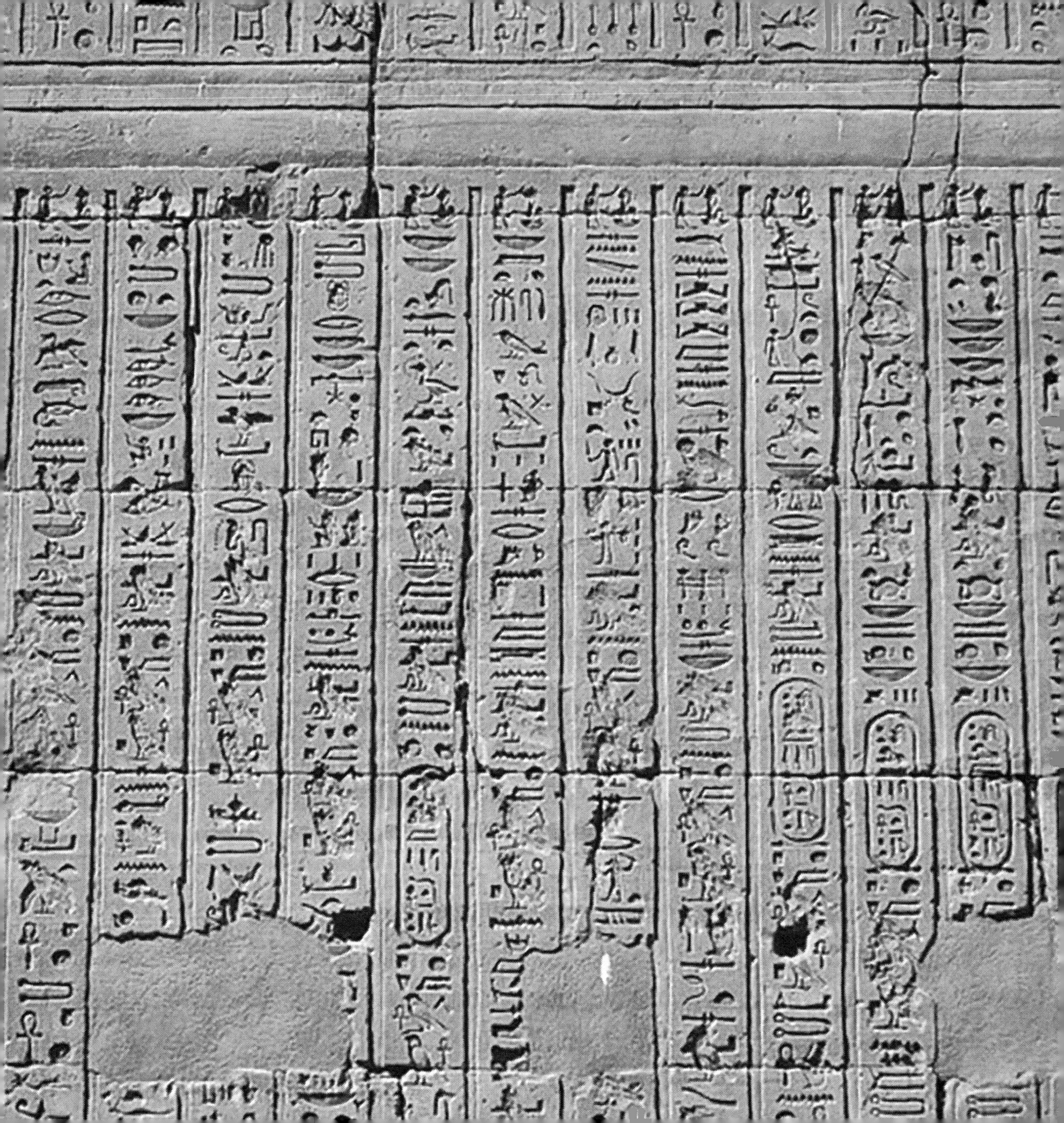

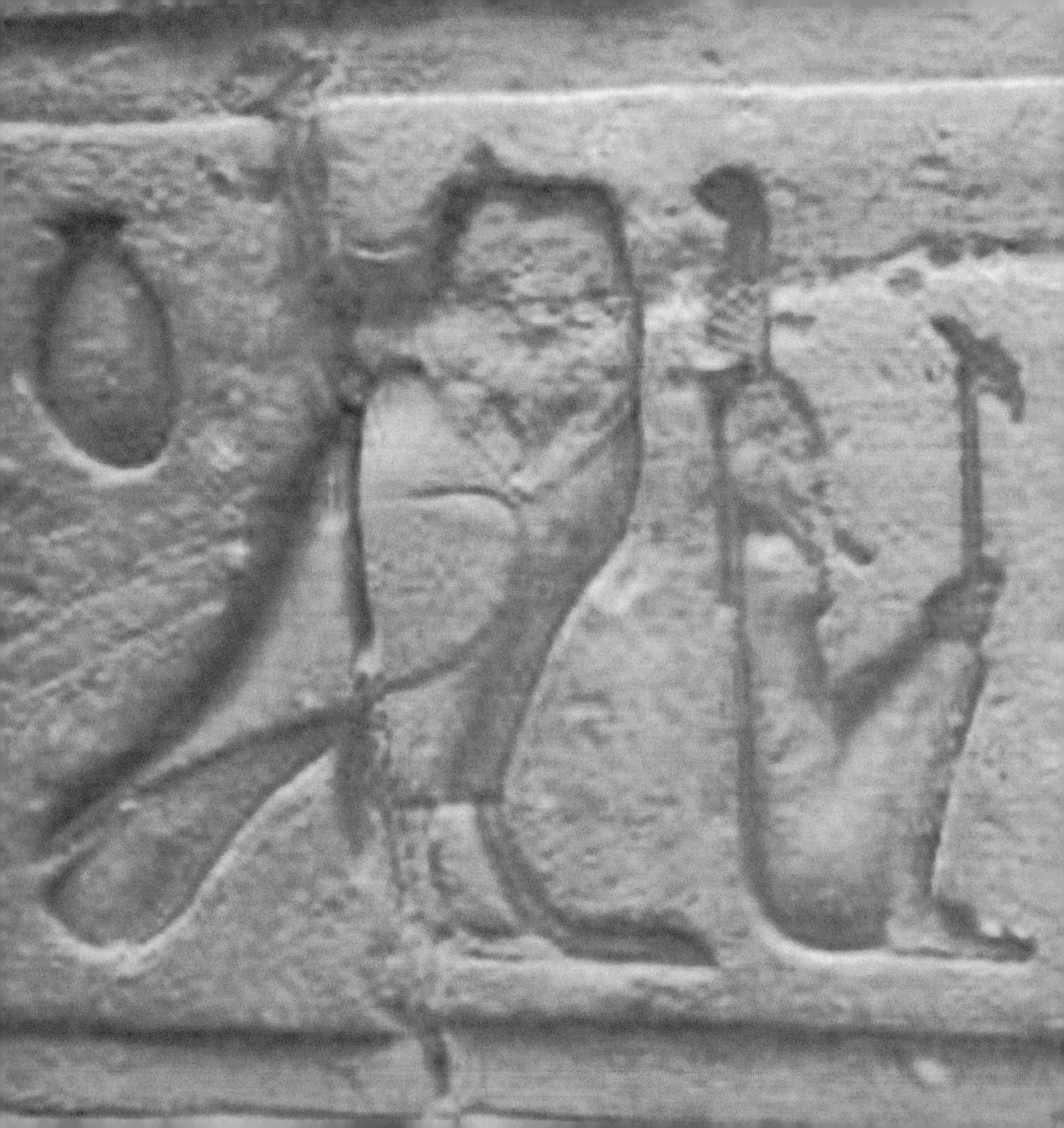

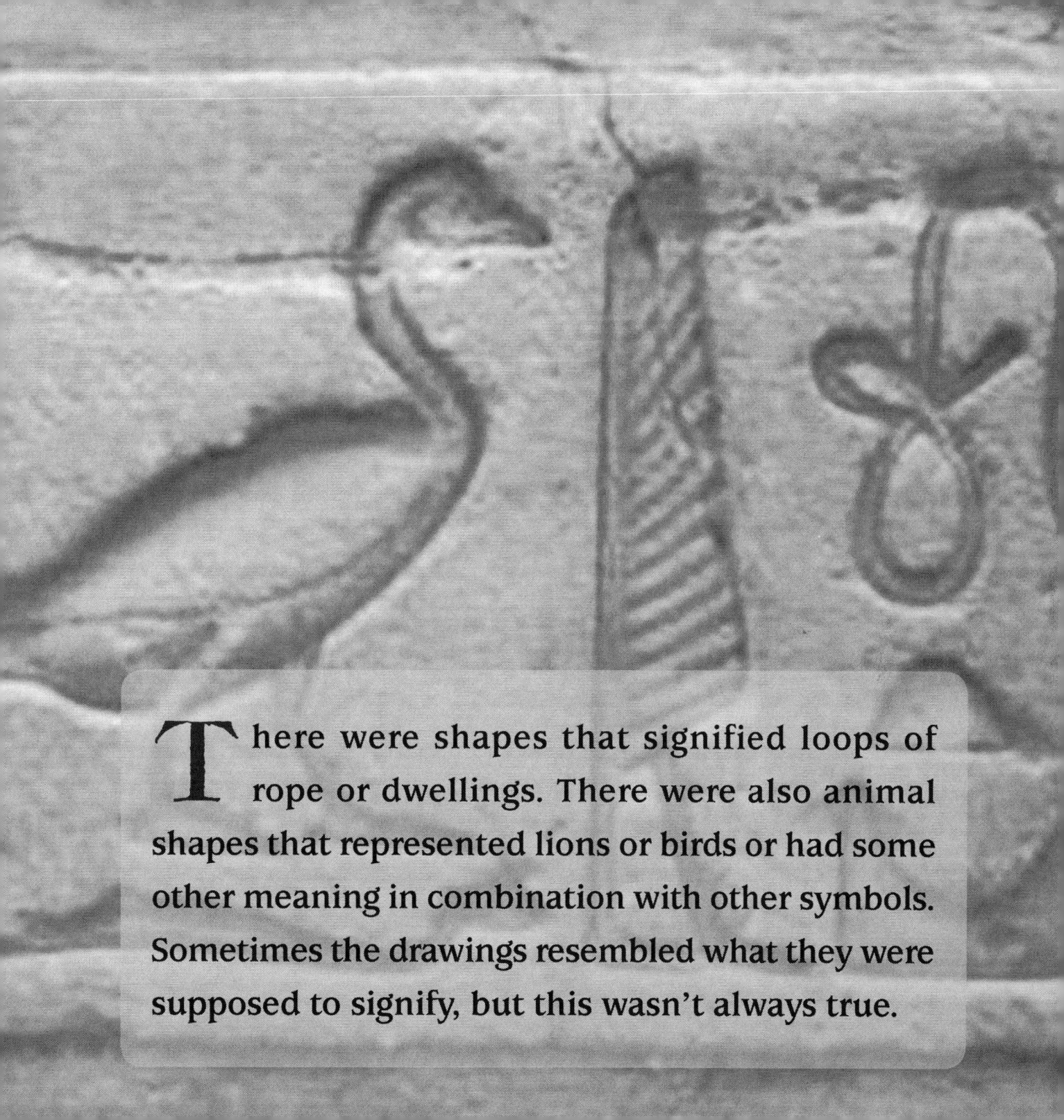

There were shapes that signified loops of rope or dwellings. There were also animal shapes that represented lions or birds or had some other meaning in combination with other symbols. Sometimes the drawings resembled what they were supposed to signify, but this wasn't always true.

In order to read and write in the Egyptian language, a scribe or priest would need years of special training beginning at the age of 12. The basic vocabulary was about 200 signs and those had to be mastered before the scribe could understand more of the language. A master scribe had knowledge of about 750 hieroglyphs. Only the most expert scribes knew 3,000 glyphs or more. Scribes were admired in the community and they became prosperous at their trade.

Scribe

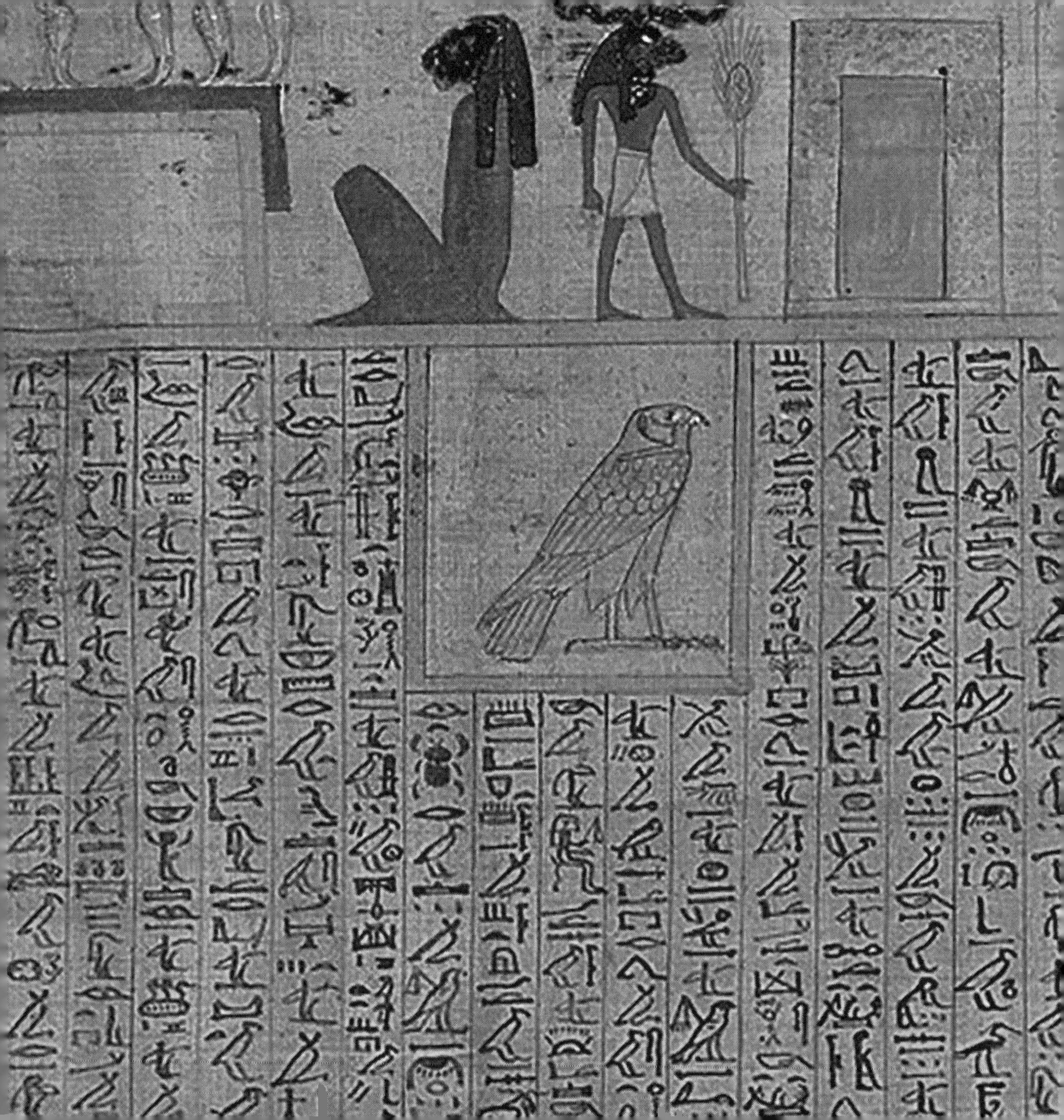

Carvers used painted inscriptions created by scribes before they engraved them in stone. The Egyptians also learned to cultivate the papyrus plant to make paper. Scribes wrote on these papyrus surfaces with special brushes made from reeds. Later on reed pens were used as well.

EGYPTIAN SCRIPT

Over many centuries, the Egyptians came up with two different types of script that they used in their writing.

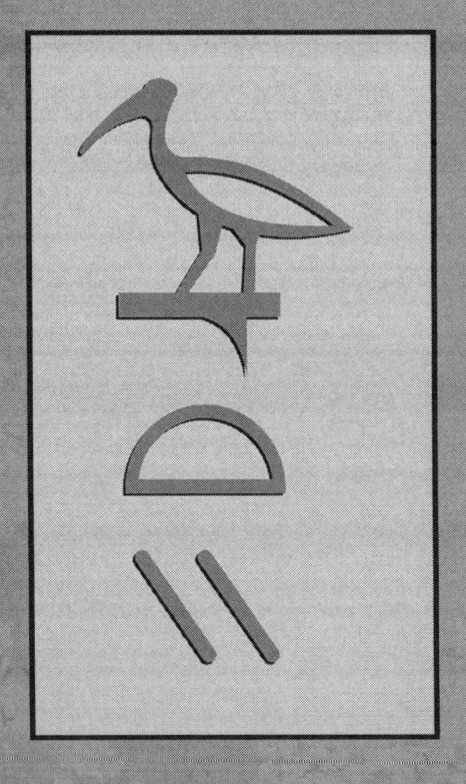

Hieratic Text

Hieratic

Hieratic was a type of hieroglyphics that used cursive script. It was less complicated than the more formal system of hieroglyphics and it had signs that were connected. Scribes used hieratic script from right to left as they wrote with brushes made of reed. They used it for official documents and letters because it was so much faster to write than standard hieroglyphics.

Demotic

Demotic script was first used about 660 BC. It was a shorthand script with symbols that didn't resemble the original glyphs. It was faster to write than standard hieroglyphics and faster than hieratic script as well.

Demotic Script

Alexander the Great

After Alexander the Great conquered Egypt for the Greeks in 332 BC, the use of glyphs began to disappear. The royal family was now Greek and most of the wealthy, elite society spoke and wrote in Greek. After the Romans conquered Egypt in 30 BC, the ancient language continued to fade. Another written form of Egyptian called Coptic began to be used. The Coptic language used about 30 signs and most of them were Greek. In most cases, a sign only represented a single sound. These Coptic signs became crucial in the deciphering of ancient hieroglyphics.

THE ROSETTA STONE

For over 1,800 years the knowledge of ancient Egyptian language was lost to the world. Many scholars had ideas for how to translate the language, but they were struggling to decipher it, because they mistakenly believe that each and every symbol represented a word. However, it turned out that hieroglyphics were much more complex than that, since a glyph can signify a word or a sound or a syllable. It can even represent an idea.

Thomas Young

Then, something amazing happened that changed everything. Napoleon invaded Egypt in the 1790s. Near the city of Rosetta, his scholars found an amazing stone. The stone had inscriptions of Greek characters as well as hieroglyphs and demotic script. Eventually, the English gained possession of the stone and a physicist by the name of Thomas Young began to decipher it in 1814.

Jean-Francois Champollion

However, it was Jean-Francois Champollion who was the first modern-day man who understood hieroglyphics. Young had found the name "Ptolemy" who was one of Egypt's rulers during the Ptolemaic dynasty. Young also figured out that not all of the glyphs represented objects or ideas and that some were sounds instead. Champollion translated the names of two other important Pharaohs—Ramesses and Thutmose. Once he had done that, he was on his way. He soon discovered the purpose of determinatives and created a dictionary that other scholars could use.

A forearm	**B** foot	**C** basket	**CH** rope	**D** hand	**E** vulture	**F** horned viper
G pot	**H** shelter	**I** reed leaf	**J** cobra	**K** basket	**L** lion	**M** owl
N water	**O** quail chick	**P** stool	**Q** hill	**R** open mouth	**S** folded cloth	**SH** lake
T bread loaf	**U** quail chick	**V** horned viper	**W** quail chick	**X** basket & folded cloth	**Y** reed leaves	**Z** door bolt

HEIROGLYPHIC CHART

Remember that the Egyptians used glyphs to represent sounds as well as ideas.

Here is a chart that shows their alphabet as closely matched to the English alphabet as possible. There are also ideograms that stand for certain letter combinations.

Here is an example of how the symbol for the ideogram for the word "tongue" could be used in different ways. The symbol for tongue is used both for meaning tongue and for the letter combination "ns."

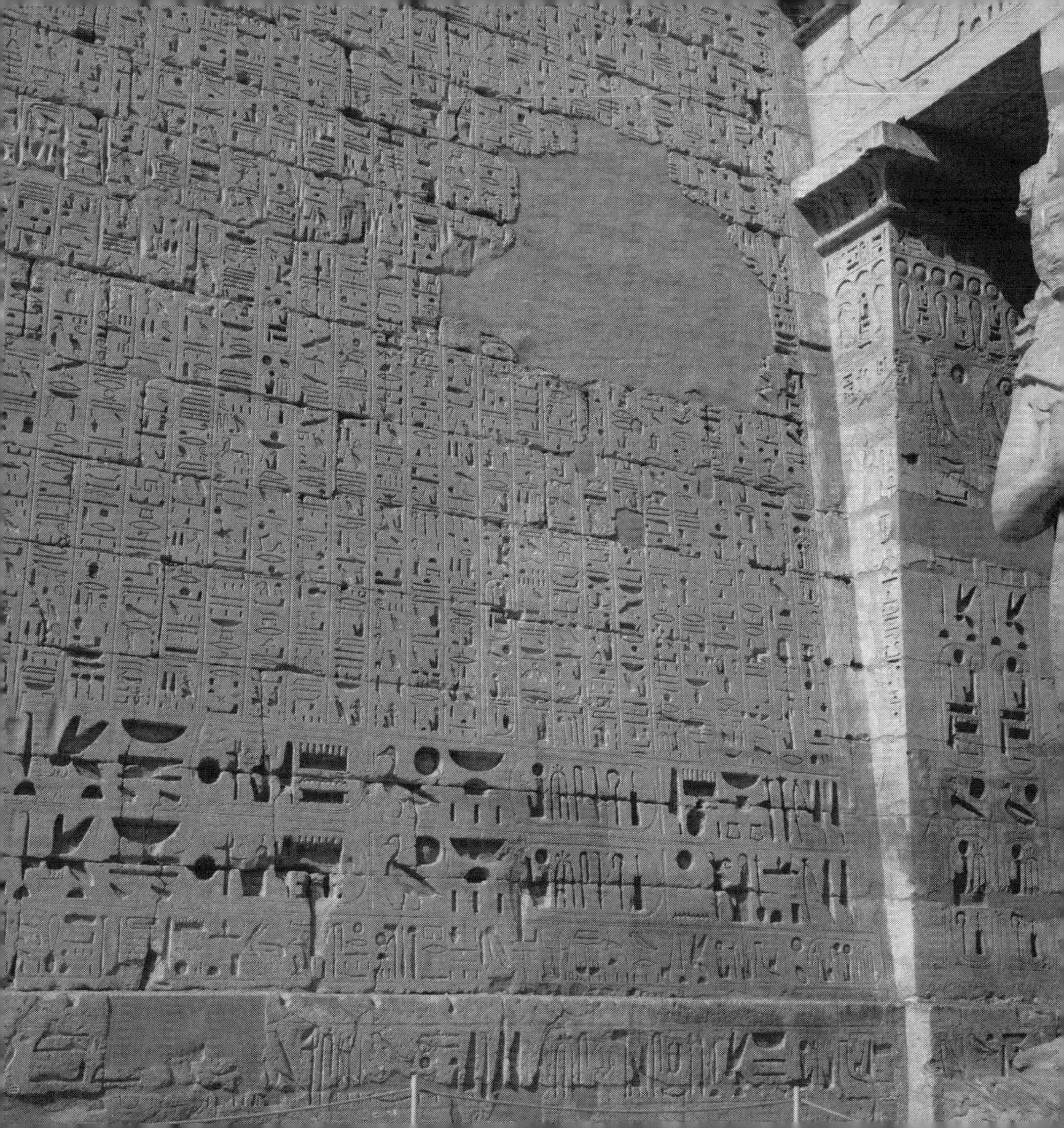

The vertical line in the ideogram is a clue that the glyph stands for one idea and not the sound version of tongue. In the phonogram, the letters "nswt" are the sounds for the word "fire," although no vowels are shown so we don't know how it was pronounced. In the determinative, the last characters are indicating that the earlier sounds of "d" and "p" are the combination that means taste. In a determinative, the final character or characters explain the earlier symbols.

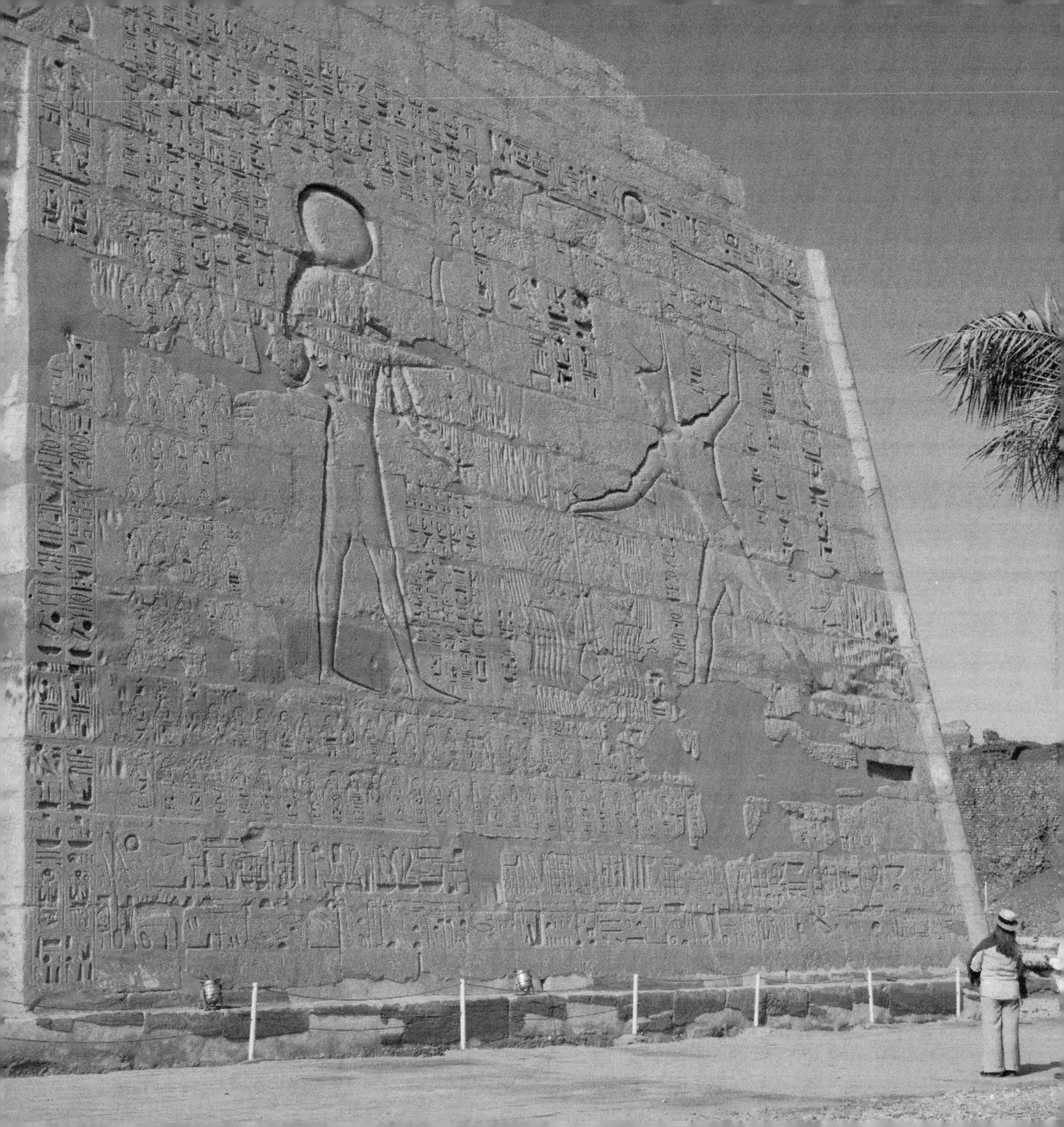

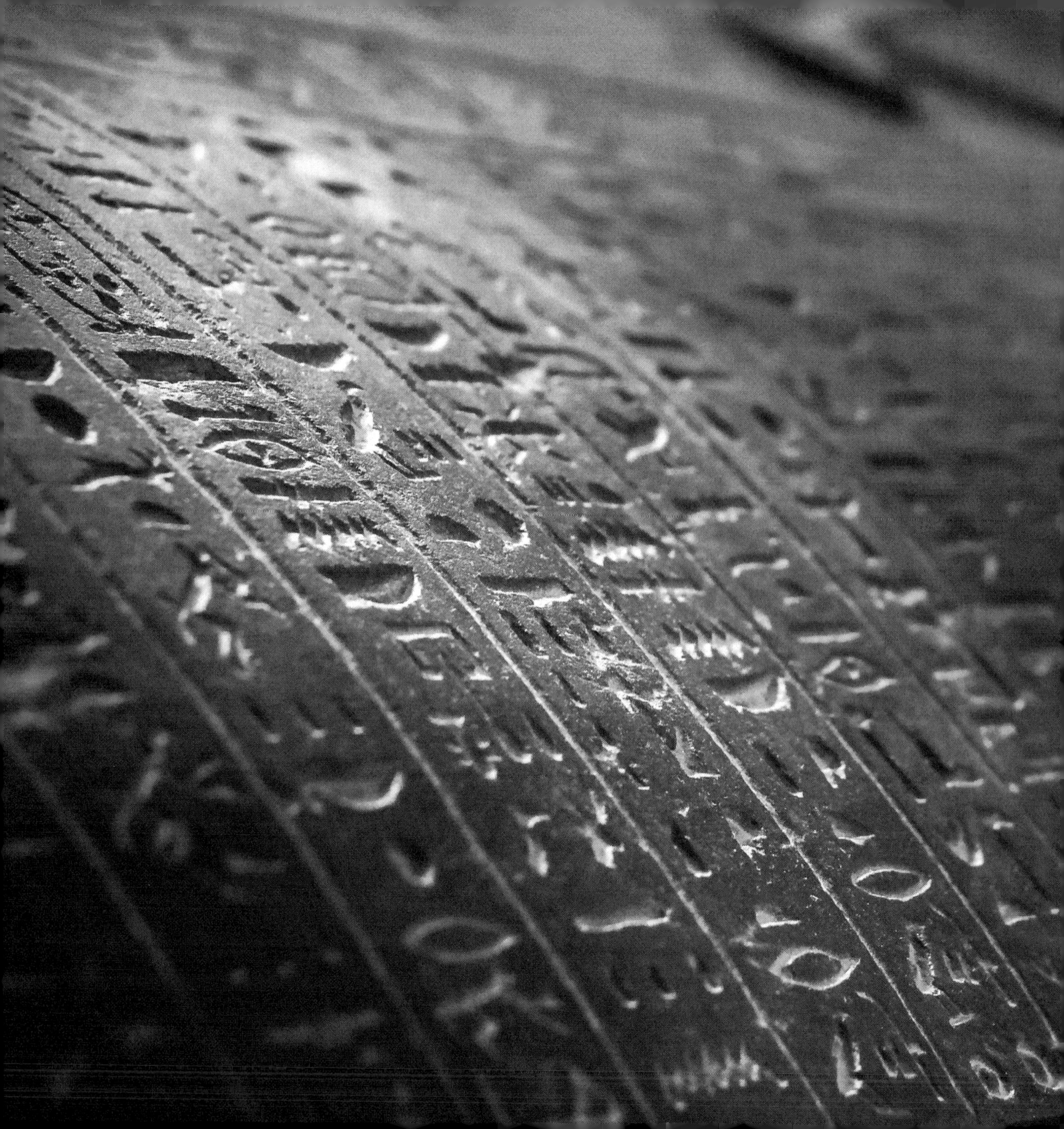

Awesome! Now you know more about Egyptian hieroglyphics. You can find more Ancient History books from Baby Professor by searching the website of your favorite book retailer.

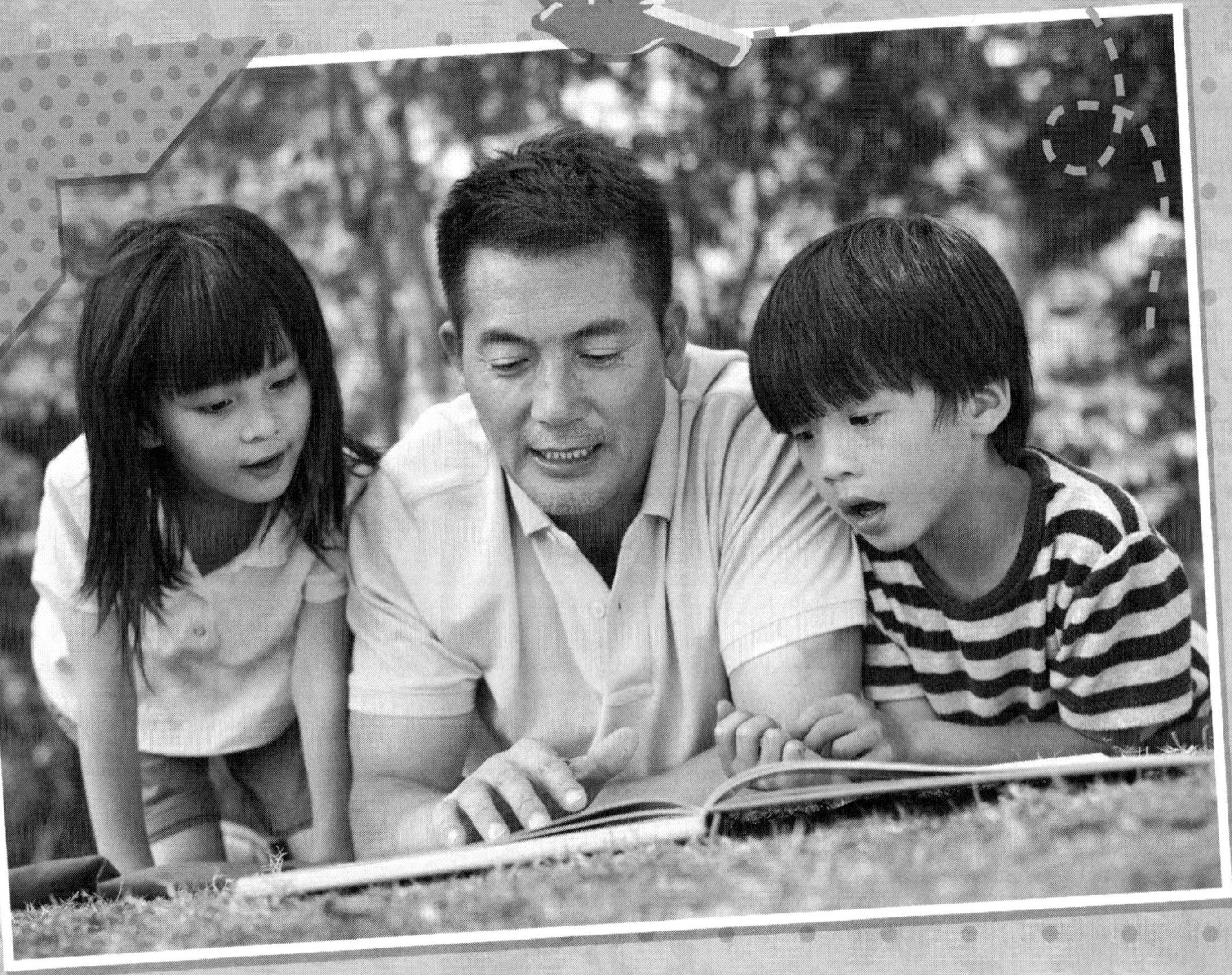

Visit

BABY PROFESSOR
EDUCATION KIDS

www.BabyProfessorBooks.com

to download Free Baby Professor eBooks
and view our catalog of new and exciting
Children's Books

Printed in Poland
by Amazon Fulfillment
Poland Sp. z o.o., Wrocław